Tom Brady

An inspiring biography of one of football's greatest players!

Table of Contents

Introduction

Thank you for taking the time to pick up this book about NFL superstar, Tom Brady!

This book aims to serve as a biography of Tom Brady, documenting his life and career to date. In the following chapters, you will learn about Brady's childhood, his high school career, his time at college, as well as all of his NFL achievements!

As you will soon discover, Tom Brady was not a natural football player. His incredible work ethic has been his key to success, and has served him well throughout the years.

Although he is now in his forties, Tom Brady is showing no signs of slowing down. Later in this book we discuss what might be next for Tom Brady, and where his career could take him after football.

Once again, thanks for choosing this book. I hope you enjoy learning about Tom Brady, and are able to draw some inspiration from his incredible life and career!

Chapter 1: Who Is Tom Brady?

Tom Brady has been the quarterback of the New England Patriots from the year 2000 until the time of writing. Since he was drafted by the Patriots, Brady has accumulated quite a shopping list of achievements, including two NFL Most Valuable Player Awards, and a still-standing record of five Super Bowl victories. To this date, no other professional football player can touch the career achievements of Tom Brady.

However, before we go into the more serious stuff about Tom Brady, here are a couple of fun factoids about him that many people don't know:

Brady was a couple of minutes late entering his first Super Bowl because he napped a bit longer than he expected

Brady wanted to have a bit more energy before entering the field in Super Bowl XXXVI, so he took a twenty-minute nap before the game. However, just 12-minutes after he dozed off, the team was already running out onto the field. Luckily for the Patriots, Brady managed to make it to the field on time, and that power nap might have helped a lot since the Patriots took home the Vince Lombardi Trophy that day.

Brady's diet regimen was not always as strict as it is now

These days, Brady's the poster boy for healthy eating, but he was not always like that. In his rookie year, Brady's diet was typical of a college fratboy; before each games he would eat a plate of nachos, his lunches would typically consist of a ham-and-cheese sub sandwich, a side of onion rings, and a tall glass of orange soda to wash all it down, and his regular dinners would be Chinese takeout or pizza.

Brady almost became a professional baseball player

Before the New England Patriots picked Brady as 199th overall
in the sixth round of the NFL Draft in 2000, Brady was also
drafted by the Montreal Expos in the 18th round of the MLB
Draft in 1995. Luckily for the Patriots, Brady did not sign with
the Expos, and instead focused on playing professional football.
Still though, one wonders what kind of a baseball player Brady
could have been.

In his rookie year, Brady was the Patriots fans' last pick to be a starting QB

In 2000, the Patriots' starting QB Drew Bledsoe's questionable
health made the team conduct a poll asking the fans who in the
current roster they would want to become the new starting
quarterback. With only 8.7% of the total vote, the rookie Tom
Brady was picked last overall to become the starting QB.

Brady has never had coffee, ever

You would have thought that with the unhealthy diet that Brady
had when he was young that he would have tried all manners of
food, but what many people are surprised to learn about the star
quarterback is that he has not had even one sip of coffee in his
entire life! Brady himself is quite puzzled about this, and has
said that he just does not feel the compulsion to try it.

Brady does not even drink Gatorade

If you thought not drinking coffee is kind of weird, then it might
just blow your mind to learn that Brady does not even drink
Gatorade during games. Instead of the widely-popular sports
drink, Brady prepares his own hydrating drink; just water with
some lemons, and a whole bunch of electrolytes, with no sugar
of course. Brady swears by this concoction; he claims that it

contains more than enough electrolytes to get him through the day without any problem.

Brady goes to bed earlier than most kids a quarter of his age

One of the things that Brady attributes to his superior athletic abilities is that he goes to bed early, as in really early. Brady is already in dreamland by 8:30 in the evening.

Drew Bledsoe hazed the rookie Brady in a fabulous manner

Hazing the rookies has been a long-kept tradition in the NFL, and the Patriots are no exception to this rule. During his rookie year, Brady was viciously pranked by the Patriots' then starting QB Drew Bledsoe. Bledsoe poured a ton of glitter into the air-conditioning vents of the rookie's car. When Brady turned on the AC of his car, he got blasted in the face with glitter.

Brady calls everyone close to him "babe", regardless of gender

It is quite a wonder that Brady has not gotten into trouble in this highly PC world, especially since he has this habit of calling every person close to him "babe", even if said person is a man. According to Brady, he picked up this habit from his dad. He actually calls everyone on the Patriots roster "babe", which is brave in itself since he is referring to more than a dozen huge, 300+ pound men using an effeminate nickname.

Brady is a serious athlete regardless of the sport

Known for being a fierce competitor on the football field, Brady is also as intense in other sports as well. For instance, Tom Brady is an avid ping-pong player, and he actually has quite a bit of skill for the game, and more than a bit of passion. As his teammates would attest, Brady's ping-pong table at home bears a lot of dents and dings resulting from him smashing his paddles in frustration whenever someone scores against him; he's kind of like the John McEnroe of table tennis in a way.

Brady is a horrible skier

Although Brady is an incredible athlete, that does not mean he excels at every sport he tries. Drew Bledsoe stated that whenever Brady would hit the slopes at the Yellowstone Club in Montana during the off-season, he would constantly put fear into the hearts of New England fans; not because he would attempt some really dangerous jumps and maneuvers, but because of how gangly and uncoordinated he was on skis. Bledsoe laments that whenever Brady straps on a pair of skis, he expects him to suffer a career-ending injury. Fortunately, this nightmare has not happened, at least not yet!

These bits of trivia are only a mere fraction of who Tom Brady is as a person. Think of this as just a sort of appetizer before you dive deeper into the life of this future Hall of Famer.

Chapter 2: The Early Years

Thomas Edward Patrick Brady Jr. was born on August 3, 1977 in San Mateo, California; the fourth and youngest child of Gallyn Patricia Johnson, and Thomas Edward Brady Sr. Tom Sr. owned a successful financial planning corporation, so you can say the family was pretty well off. Tom was the youngest of the four Brady siblings, and the only boy.

The Brady family lived in San Mateo, California, a county located on the southern peninsula of San Francisco, around thirty minutes away from the downtown area. San Mateo is the polar opposite of the slums where many of today's athletes used to live. In fact, it is actually one of the 20 most affluent counties in the entire United States. Some of the homes in the tree-lined street where the Brady's lived were mansions whose driveways were almost always full of luxury vehicles.

Even though he lived a comfortable, Tom Brady did not let all of this get to his head. Brady's work ethic rivaled, and maybe even surpassed, all of the professional football players in the NFL. Even when he was just a young boy, he would practice for hours pitching and batting (his first real sport was actually baseball). He never let his comfortable life turn him into a lazy, unmotivated bum. He let his ambitions for sports greatness fuel him.

Living In the Shadows of His Sisters

Young Tommy Brady was as straight-laced as they come; he collected baseball cards by the boxful, was an altar boy at the local Catholic church, and enjoyed fishing. Even as a young kid, Brady displayed exceptional arm strength when he was flinging rolled-up newspapers onto their neighbor's lawns from the back of his mom's Volkswagen Van. However, he was not the star athlete in the family back then.

One might think that being in a home full of girls would mean that the family was not that inclined towards sports, but one would be wrong. Although Tom Sr. and Galynn tried to steer their kids towards fine arts and music, all four of them gravitated towards sports, and they went on to become accomplished athletes in their hometown. Maureen, the oldest of the four Brady kids, was a star softball pitcher, who managed to make it on the U.S. Junior Olympic Team when she was just 17. Maureen also got a sports scholarship at the Fresno State University.

Julie, the second eldest, was a great soccer player and also got an athletic scholarship. The third Brady kid, Nancy, was also an accomplished softball player like Maureen, and she also got an athletic scholarship into UCLA-Berkeley, but she decided to go on an entirely different path away from sports.

As a kid, Tom Brady was always mentioned as the younger brother of his sister Maureen, which was understandable as she was the star athlete of the town. However, Tom did not just sit back and watch as his sisters dominated athletically over him. Maureen recalls that Tom once wrote an essay for school where he mentioned that he was tired of being called the younger brother of Maureen Brady. He prophetically stated that he will be so famous one day that he will be able to turn the tables; one day, the elder Brady siblings will henceforth be known as Tom Brady's sisters. Their mother also remembered back when Tom was a young kid, he told her that Tom Brady would one day become a household name.

Tom never really minded that he grew up with no brothers, in fact, he liked it. According to Brady, he liked being the only boy since he did not have to share his clothes with anyone, he did not have to play with hand-me-down toys, and he liked the attention he got from his sister's friends when they came to the house. Sure, there were times when the older girls took advantage of little Tommy Brady; like when they made him wear a dress, and when they painted his nails. Jokes aside, Tom Brady's sisters truly did love him and they assured him that they always had his back with whatever he chose to do. When Brady began his football journey in Junipero Serra High School, which was quite a lackluster couple of years for the All-star QB, his sisters provided him with a sort of emotional cocoon to protect him from all the disappointments that came his way.

Tom Brady also got to spend quite a lot of time with his dad, Tom Sr. in fact, it was the elder Brady that instilled the love of all sports in the future football phenom. Tom Sr. and Jr. would spend most of their Sunday afternoons on the golf course, and when Brady got seriously interested in football, his dad would take him on visits to out-of-state training camps.

Tom Brady grew up in a very loving family, which made him into the most down-to-earth, clean-cut, and straight-laced professional athlete that you will ever see.

Growing Up in a Sports-crazy Home

Even though Tom Sr. and Gallyn wanted their children to pursue the classical arts, it does not, by any means mean that the family was averse to sports. In fact, the entire family was crazy about sports, football in particular.

The Brady's, for 20 years bought season tickets for the 49ers. Tom Brady fondly remembers all those years when he would watch his idol, Joe Montana from the tenth to the last row in Candlestick Park. In fact, in 1981, when Tom was still 4-years-old, the whole Brady family was in Candlestick Park when Joe Montana managed to pull off the miraculous play that is known today as simply "The Catch". Tom Brady likely did not feel as elated as the rest of the people in the stadium were back then. According to his mom, Brady cried for the entire first half of the game, only stopping during the second half after his dad brought him one of those huge foam hands.

To this day, the entire Brady family, Tom included, still worship Joe Montana. In fact, no one in the family dares to think of Tom as being the next Joe Montana, because for them, it would be sacrilegious to do so.

Early Disappointments in Sport

When you look at where Tom Brady is now and all of the achievements he has had so far, you would think that he was a natural-born athlete; someone who was in the limelight for the better part of his young life. That is not really the case, actually, it is not even close to what Brady had to go through.

What made Tom Brady a great athlete was not his natural talent, but his unwavering optimism, superhuman work ethic, and his unquenchable thirst to become better. If any normal person experienced all of the things that Brady did during his early years, he or she would have likely quit long before reaching their true potential.

During those early years, nobody would have thought that Tom was the athlete in the family, but that would soon change.

Today, in the Brady's old family home, which is where Maureen and her family resides, aside from the Patriots flag waving in front of the house, you will not find any evidence that it was once the home of one of the NFL's greatest players. Inside the house, you will also not find any shrine to the great football player. What you will find though are awkward family photos that include the young Tommy Brady.

Chapter 3: High School Football

After graduating from St. Gregory School where he attended elementary and middle school, Tom Brady enrolled in one of the big name high schools in San Mateo: Junipero Serra High School. Serra is an exclusive all-boys high school that mostly caters to upper middle-class families. Tom Brady had high hopes for himself the moment that he set foot on the grounds of Serra, but what he did not know back then was that the road ahead would be quite rough and full of obstacles.

Brady as a baseball player

Many fans would be surprised to know that football was not the only sport that Tom Brady played as a high school student. Tom Brady also became the catcher for the Junipero Serra high school junior varsity baseball team; and he was quite a skilled player too.

Just like his sisters before him, young Tommy Brady grew up playing softball and baseball, and he also had quite a successful run at Little League, which is why the school had high hopes for the youngest Brady to join the baseball team; and he did.

Dean Ayoob was a senior when Tom Brady was a freshman at Serra high school, and he is now the school's athletic director. According to Ayoob, it was not Brady's skills that made him stand out as a baseball player, it was his work ethic and his die hard obsession to prepare his body for every game. Ayoob says that Brady was geared more towards playing baseball as this was the sport that he had more experience in, and back then he did not really have the physicality to be a football player.

During the two seasons when Tom Brady played for the Serra baseball team, he hit .311, hit eight home runs, 11 double plays, and had 44 RBI in 61 games. His outstanding stats earned Brady the status of All-league catcher during his senior year.

Tom Brady was such a good high school baseball player that several pro teams expressed interest in drafting the young man straight out of high school. One team, the Montreal Expos, actually followed through with their interests and tried to draft Tom Brady in 1995.

Tom Brady actually had quite a couple of notable exploits while in the diamond, including hitting a home run clear over the fence and into the parking lot, hitting the team's bus and waking up their driver. Another story of Brady's excellence as a baseball player tells of how he managed to hit a homerun in the Seattle Kingdome using a wooden bat when he was participating at a pre-draft workout.

Legend has it that Brady's receivers when he was in high school could hear the ball whizz through the air whenever they made their cuts. Brady could easily throw out base runners going to second base with his powerful throwing arm.

Tom Brady and the Montreal Expos

One of the biggest "what ifs" in modern sports is "what if Tom Brady took the Expos' offer?" Should the GOAT agree to joining Major League Baseball, would it have made a difference? Kevin Malone, the former general manager of the Expos recalled the time when he took a liking to the future NFL Hall of Famer.

Tom Brady's infamously poor football scouting report was and always will be the NFL's biggest missed opportunity. However, his baseball scouting reports were much more positive. They were so good in fact, that other baseball players would kill to have them. Malone, in his words, sent Brady "a flier", but the young high-schooler had his eyes set on being a football player.

What Malone liked in Brady, aside from his size and athleticism, was his face. He had what Malone calls, a "major league face". Even back then, Brady had an athletic, strong body, but Malone said that he still had a lot of room for improvement. Malone knew that the Expos could help Brady improve and learn how to better receive and call a game, and he honestly felt that young

Tommy had good instincts as a baseball player. However, the Expos knew that signing Brady to join was a longshot, which is why they did not use up their top picks and drafted him quite a way down the draft pool.

Could Brady have helped the Expos?

The Expos had the best record in the league in 1994, but the player's strike preemptively ended an erstwhile impressive season and cancelled the World Series; it signaled the end of the Expos, in Motreal at least. The team suffered from financial difficulties, which forced a number of their players, including Pedro Martinez and Larry Walker, to bail out and find other teams to play for. Eventually, when a stadium deal failed to fall through, the MLB bought the Expos' franchise and the team migrated to Washington where it got rebranded into the Nationals in 2004.

Kevin Malone agrees that should Brady have signed up with the team, and the player strike of 94 did not happen, baseball history might have taken a different course, and it might have even kept the Expos in Montreal.

No matter how talented Brady was at baseball, he somehow knew that it was not the sport that was meant for him. Tom Brady declined the multi-million-dollar deal with the Expos, and focused on playing college football instead.

Brady's High School Football Career

Football has always been Brady's true love, but during his high school days, it seemed like his love was a one-way street. You would think that as great as Tom Brady is now, that he would have been the star player of the Junipero Serra Padres the moment he joined the team, but you would be wrong.

During his freshman year as a junior varsity player for Serra, Tom Brady was the back-up for the back-up quarterback of the team. He was so low in the pecking order that he would rarely get any playing time per game, if any at all. This is actually saying something as the Serra football team was 0-8 the previous year, and did not score a single touchdown the entire season.

During his early days in high school, Tom Brady was not the powerhouse player that he is now; quite the opposite in fact. Although he had a strong throwing arm, he was so slow on his feet. Brady admits that while he is still a slow runner right now, he was much worse when he was in high school.

Brady finally got his chance to become the starting quarterback for the Padres in his junior year, when the main quarterback got injured and could not finish the rest of the season. Somehow, Brady convinced the head coach to pick him to be the new starting QB. From that day on, until Brady graduated high school, he did not give up his starting position. Although Brady back then was kind of skilled, he still had some difficulty getting the attention of talent scouts from the different universities.

Chapter 4: Brady's Collegiate Experience

After turning down the Expos' offer, Tom Brady fixed his sights on getting into a good college through a football player's scholarship, but it was easier said than done.

Despite helping the Junipero High School Padres finish 11-20 in a rugged high school league, the college scouts hardly took notice of Tom Brady, which is a trend that would continue later on in his career. Brady knew that if he wanted to attend the college he wanted, he needed to act on his own. With the help of his dad, Brady created highlight reels of his high school games and attached them in his college applications. This helped him land a scholarship to the University of Michigan.

Brady's Freshman Year

No one really expected great things from Tom Brady when he first played football for the Wolverines. He looked just like any other wannabe professional football player, and he was not that athletic at all. One analyst said that you could time Tom Brady's 40-yard dash with a calendar, in other words, he was born with cement blocks for feet. In addition, when he was drafted by Michigan, Brady was seventh in the depth chart; this means that there were six other quarterbacks picked before him.

Brady's freshman year in Michigan was quite lackluster; he was the backup quarterback and rarely experienced any play time. In fact, Brady's first time off the bench was quite a disaster. The Wolverines were already well on their way to a blow out victory, and during trash time the head coach finally allowed Brady on the field. Brady dusted off his helmet and stepped onto the field with just a couple of minutes on the clock and the Wolverines up by an impossible amount. Once the ball was snapped to Brady, the other team's defense all came crashing on him. In a fit of panic, Brady managed to throw the ball before he got sacked, unfortunately, his pass got intercepted and got converted into a touchdown. This horrible first play at the college bowl still haunts Brady to this day, and he says he will not forget that game for the rest of his life.

To say that Brady's first year as a Wolverine was lackluster would be an understatement. For the entire 96 season, Brady threw a total of five passes, with only three of them actually completed.

Brady's Sophomore year

Brady's second year as a Wolverine was a bit more challenging than his first. As a sophomore, he was the backup quarterback for the team's star, future NFL player Brian Griese. Just like his first year, Brady rarely made it on the field, however he did manage to throw a bit more this year than the previous.

Brady threw a total of fifteen passes during the 97 season, and he managed to complete twelve of them.

Brady the Junior

At the start of the '98 season, Brady managed to convince the head coach that he was worthy of being the starting quarterback; Brian Griese was drafted by the Denver Broncos in the third round. Lloyd Carr, the head coach of the Wolverines back then, gave in to Brady's requests, as he saw that the young man had an almost supernatural drive to get better.

However, even though Brady became the starting QB and the team captain, this was the year that the University of Michigan would alienate and bash him; and this left quite deep wounds in Brady, wounds that would take a lot of years to heal, almost 20 years in fact, but more on that story later.

Brady's junior year almost became his last. The Wolverines won the national championship that year. On autograph day, fans of the Wolverines lined up outside the stadium to get the signatures of their favorite players. Although Brady was the team captain and contributed much to the victory of the team, the fans all went to the freshman phenom Drew Henson. It was clear that the fans all wanted Henson to be the starting quarterback.

Drew Henson was a Michigan native, and one of the top recruits of the college. All of these factors combined to make him a fan favorite over Brady. In fact, even though Brady had a stellar season during his junior year, Lloyd Carter still split his playing time with Henson. However, Brady did not let this setback get him down; Brady worked even harder at improving himself. He viewed and reviewed the tapes of their prior games, multiple times until he almost memorized all of the other teams' moves and strategies. This was when Brady developed his "clairvoyant" ability to recognize defensive plays.

However, Henson had a lot of raw talent within him. There was a time when Henson stopped playing football for awhile because a Major League baseball team drafted him, and he left to play with them briefly. When Henson returned, even without playing football for almost a year, he quickly caught up to Brady.

Brady actually though about transferring schools back then. The fans and the entire school treating him badly really did not help with his anxiety problems and low self-esteem. Brady told Carr that he wanted to transfer back to Cal, as he was frankly unhappy with his playing time and he seriously doubted if his career would advance should he stay in Michigan. Instead of coddling him, coach Carr told him that he should go back to his apartment and sleep on his decision and they would talk the following day.

During the course of that conversation, Carr told Brady that if Brady was truly serious about transferring schools, he would be more than happy to oblige and sign his release papers. However, Carr told the young Brady that leaving Michigan would be the biggest mistake he would make in his life. Carr said, "Look, you're in a very competitive situation here. All you guys have talent. The best advice I can give anybody in a competitive situation is that they come in here every single day prepared mentally and physically to compete at their very best. Don't be watching the other guy hoping he has a bad day or doesn't do well. Just worry about getting better every day." The following day, Brady marched into Carr's office and declared that he had decided to stay in Michigan and prove to him that he can be a great quarterback.

 "Getting better every day" has since become Brady's mantra that he's followed for his entire college and professional career.

Brady's final year as a Wolverine

The start of Brady's final season in Michigan got off to a rough start. With Griese gone, coach Carr appointed Brady to the starting quarterback position, but the fans and most of the college administration still wanted hotshot freshman Drew Henson. Things did not really go Brady's way, especially when Brady was booed by the Michigan crowd off the field when the Wolverines lost their opening game against Syracuse.

Aside from the fans, lots of other sources were putting pressure on the University of Michigan Wolverines to give Drew Henson more game time. George Steinbrenner of the New York Yankees had already offered Henson a $2-million signing bonus, and the Ohio State Buckeyes also expressed their interest in getting Henson to play for their squad. Coach Carr had no other choice but to once again split the playing time between Henson and Brady. Technically, Brady would still be the starting quarterback, but Henson would play the second quarter, and then Carr would decide which of the two would play for the entire second half.

True to his word, Tom Brady worked his butt off to earn his status as starting quarterback. Whenever he felt that Henson was getting close to his position, Brady would work twice as hard to convince Coach Carr that he should be the starting QB for the Wolverines, and in his last season as a Wolverine, Brady started in all of the games.

Chapter 5: Taking The NFL By Storm

Although Tom Brady worked hard on his strength and conditioning when he was in Michigan, he was still a tall, stringy, 20-year-old when he entered the 2000 NFL Draft. Getting the attention of college scouts was difficult enough, but catching the eye of the scouts of professional NFL teams would prove to be much more difficult as Tom Brady would soon find out.

Flying Under the Radar of the NFL

The odds were piled high against Tom Brady in the Draft Class of 2000. For one thing, Brady was still painfully slow. His fastest time at the 40-yard dash was a piddling 5.2 seconds, much slower than what was expected for an effective quarterback back then. In the entire rookie combine, Brady was the slowest quarterback, and only three other people in the whole thing ran slower than he did. In addition, although Brady had a strong and accurate throwing arm, he sorely lacked in strength and bulk.

Suffice to say, many teams in the NFL flat out ignored Tom Brady, which caused the New England Patriots to grab the biggest steal of all time. However, the Patriots themselves almost did not draft Brady.

Why Did the Patriots Draft Brady so Late?

This did not mean that the Patriots had absolutely no interest in getting Brady, quite the opposite actually. However, a couple of factors made them rethink their decision to get the future GOAT in the squad.

First, the entire Patriots organization was in quite a mess that year. The Pats lost six of their final eight games in the '99 season, and they had just fired the former head coach Pete Carroll, and hired Bill Bellichick in his place.

Second, the Patriots were already $10.5-million over the NFL's salary cap and they had 42 players on the roster. To get themselves within the salary cap, the Pats had to shave down their numbers to 39 players.

Lastly, for the 2000 season, the last thing that the New England Patriots needed was another quarterback. The team's projected roster of 39 players were already ideal, because that meant they could have three quarterbacks. In addition, the Patriots still had Drew Bledsoe, who at 28 years old was still at the prime of his athleticism.

Before the draft started, Belichick sent the Pats' quarterback coach Dick Rehbein to search for worthwhile QBs that they could add to the roster. When Rehbein returned after touring the entire countryside, he told Belichick that Tom Brady from the UM Wolverines seemed like the best fit for the team's system. Surprisingly, many of the other coaches and those in the front office of the Pats also agreed.

If the Patriots were genuinely interested in drafting Brady the why did they wait until the sixth round to get him? The answer was the Patriots were picking rookies strategically; they first picked players that they knew they needed before taking players that they somewhat liked. Scott Pioli, the Patriots' general manager at the time, said that they started thinking of getting Brady as early as the third round of drafting. However, they had to do things strategically so they put Brady on the backburner. Once the sixth round started, Pioli noticed that Brady was still there, so he thought to himself "Everyone liked him, what are we doing?" so he decided to pick Tom Brady; the 199th pick in the 6th round of drafting in the rookie class of 2000. This would signal the beginning of the legendary Patriots team that would make it to the Super Bowl three times in the next four years, and winning all of them.

Brady's First Years as a Patriot

In his rookie year, Tom Brady suffered through the same ordeal that plagued him during his first high school and college years; he was benched and served as the backup for Drew Bledsoe, who was the first overall pick of the 1993 NFL Draft. Under Bledsoe, the Patriots ended their seven-season post-season drought, made the semis four times, and appeared in the Super Bowl once. This made it unlikely for Brady, who was just a scraggly rookie to start a game, let alone play.

There's a story going around about the first time that the Patriots' owner Robert Kraft first met Tom Brady. Brady, with a pizza box under one arm, approached Kraft to shake his hand. Kraft back then mixed Tom with another Brady in the roster, but then he remembered that this young man in front of him was the team's sixth round pick. Instead of feeling put down, Kraft remembered that Brady told him that yes, he was the Pats' sixth round pick, adding "and I'm the best decision this organization has ever made." Brady really followed through with his prophetic promise.

During the Patriots' second game for the 2001 season against the New York Jets, at the 4:48 mark of the 4th quarter, the Jets' linebacker, Mo Lewis, delivered a brutal sideline hit that knocked the wind out of Bledsoe and rendered him unconscious for a couple of minutes. It turned out that Bledsoe suffered from a severed blood vessel inside his chest, and it proceeded to fill his chest cavity with blood. Bledsoe was rushed away in an ambulance. Belichick had no other option but to let Tom Brady replace Bledsoe for the rest of the game.

In his first game in the NFL, Brady managed to gain a couple of yards as the replacement QB. That was enough to convince Belichick that Brady was the perfect choice for starting QB. Although Bledsoe was cleared to come back to play, and he did so for a single series and managed to throw one pass, the Patriots decided to make Brady the permanent starter.

Brady's First Trip to the Super Bowl

Talk about making the best of what you get, as that is exactly what Tom Brady did the moment he became the starting quarterback of the Patriots. It almost seemed like destiny that Bledsoe got sidelined early in the season, because the next game for the Patriots, and the first with Brady at the helm, was against the Indianapolis Colts and Peyton Manning, who would become Brady's top rival in the game.

Even without Bledsoe, the Patriots absolutely decimated the Colts on that day, the final score being 44-13. Even though Brady did a pretty good job at the quarterback position, throwing a total of 168 yards with 13 completed passes from 23 attempts, it was a total team effort, especially the defense team that managed to lock down Manning, intercepting three of his passes.

According to Mark Rypien, who was Manning's backup quarterback that day, he did not see anything special in Tom Brady; to him, Brady was just another young buck, who had a bit of talent for being a quarterback. However, he did admit that he admired Brady's ability to extend plays in the pocket. It was as if Brady knew already how the defense would react, and he would side-step or step back at exactly the right time to escape them.

That win against the Indianapolis Colts was the first for the Pats that season, and it also signaled the start of one of the greatest stretches in the NFL. The Patriots would then proceed to breeze through the next 14 regular season games, losing only three more times, ending the regular season with an 11-5 record; the Patriots continued to win the semis, become division champions, and then face and defeat the St. Louis Rams in Superbowl XXXVI to snatch the franchise's first ever Vince Lombardi trophy.

2001 was the year that the NFL and its fans would first learn about the legend that is Tom Brady.

Brady's Five Superbowl Rings

No one, not even Tom Brady's own family, could have predicted that he would lead the New England Patriots to the Superbowl in his second season with the team, much less lead the team to eight more Superbowls, winning 4 of them, for a total of 5 championship rings.

As mentioned earlier, the Patriots won Superbowl XXXVI against the St. Louis Rams. At the Superbowl XXXVIII in 2003, Brady and the Patriots defeated the Carolina Panthers. The following year, in Superbowl XXXIX, the Pats defeated the Philadelphia Eagles. In 2014, after an almost ten-year championship drought, the Patriots defeated the Seattle Seahawks in Superbowl XLIX. In 2016, at Superbowl LI, the Patriots won against the Atlanta Falcons in a heated overtime battle.

With five Superbowl rings, Tom Brady is the quarterback who has won the most NFL championships in his career, actually beating his idols Joe Montana and Terry Bradshaw. At the time of writing, Tom Brady has just turned 40 years old, but he is yet to show any signs of slowing down. Who knows, there might still be enough fight in him to get one more, maybe even two more, championship rings before he retires.

Chapter 6: Notable Achievements

In his almost 18-year long career, it is only normal for Tom Brady to have accumulated quite a lot of awards and accomplishments in the National Football League. Being a true underdog since the day he was drafted in the sixth round, the franchise player of the Patriots is continuously working hard every day to make himself even better.

From 2000 to 2018, Tom Brady has:

- Won fifteen division titles with the same team that drafted him, the New England Patriots

- Eight of those fifteen division championships were converted into AFC Championships, and then into Super Bowl appearances.

- Has the most number of Super Bowl appearances for an active player.

- Has won five Super Bowls, and is tied with Charles Hayley for the most championships by a single player.

- Has the most Super Bowl wins with a single team.

- Has the most Super Bowl MVP Awards [Super Bowls XXXVI (2001), XXXVIII (2004) and XLIX (2015)]

- Has the most post-season wins by a quarterback of all time with a record of 27-10.

- Has more appearances in playoff games than any other player before him, with 37 games, and he also started in all of them, which is a separate record on its own

- Has the most playoff wins by a starting quarterback, with 27 games won

- Has the record for most completed passes in the playoffs with 920

- Holds the record for most touchdown passes in the Super Bowl with 18

- Holds the record for the most consecutive completions in a single Super Bowl (Super Bowl XLVI with 16)

- Has won three NFL MVP awards.

- Has won the Comeback Player of the Year (2009)

- Has the highest combined regular and post-season win total for a quarterback in all of professional football history

- Is the oldest quarterback to lead the league in passing yards

- Holds the best touchdown to interception ratio for a full season with 28:2

- Has the third best career passing rating in history with 97.9

- Has the third best yards thrown in his lifetime with 66,159

Chapter 7: Controversies And Scandals

Tom Brady, with all his success and achievements, has not been immune to controversies in his football career. Although Brady tries to maintain a clean-cut, straight-laced image, there are some times when a small slip-up results in a lot of rumors about him; and when you are someone as big as Tom Brady, even the smallest issues will surely be blown way out of proportion.

Please take note that this book does not aim to defend Tom Brady's misdemeanors, surely there are a number of issues about this legendary quarterback that are no doubt true. However, we will only be covering the scandals at face value for now. If you want to dig deeper, there are tons of news articles written about Brady over the years that will provide you with plenty of reading material to do so.

Spygate

One of the biggest scandals that Tom Brady, and the entire New England Patriots organization has been involved in was back in 2007, when an assistant for the Patriots was caught videotaping the New York Jets defensive team's hand signals.

To make it clear, the scouts of the teams in the league are allowed to occupy the press box seats to gain information about their team's next two opponents. However, they are only allowed to take still pictures and talk into a voice recorder. This means that they have to figure out what kind of offensive or defensive play the coaches are making and then describe the hand signals that they are making. This is terribly difficult work, and usually, the information the scouts gather is only somewhat helpful. Video taping the other team's bench is another thing altogether, because it will allow the opposing team to thoroughly examine the signals and implement solutions against the play.

Videotaping the opponent's bench is not illegal, technically, since scouts are allowed to do so from a predetermined location. However, what the scout of the Patriots did was take video at the opponent's sideline. In addition, the camera used had a small, but very powerful microphone, so it was able to capture clear audio of the conversations in the huddle.

After some serious investigation, the NFL Commissioner Roger Goodell found the New England Patriots and their head coach were in violation of league rules. Goodell stated that the "spying" was a premeditated and calculated attempt at avoiding the leagues rules designed to promote fair play and honest competition among the teams on the playing field.

The NFL slapped Bill Belichick with a stiff fine of $500,000, which is the maximum amount allowed by the league, and at the time, the largest fine ever placed on a head coach of an NFL team. The Patriots organization also got a $250,000 fine, and the NFL also stripped the team of their original first-round pick in the 2008 Draft. Should the Patriots not get fined, they would have gotten the 31st pick of the first round. The media had a field day with the sanctions imposed on the Patriots, mainly because of the maximum fine slapped on Belichick.

The NFL required the Patriots organization to turn over all of the video tapes and related documents about their opponents' hand signals. However, the Pats did not want the said tapes to leave their facility. Goodell then proceeded to send league officials directly to the Patriots training facility where they proceeded to destroy the tapes. US Senator, Arlen Specter, criticized this rather extreme move ordered by the NFL, so he ordered Goodell to meet with him and explain the circumstances behind the move. On February 13, 2008, after his meeting with Roger Goodell, Senator Specter reported that Goodell said that Bill Belichick has been illegally videotaping the Pats' opponents ever since he became the team's head coach back in 2000. However, in his defense, Belichick said he thought that he was not breaking any rules since he was not recording and using the tapes on the same game.

In connection to this scandal, a former St. Louis Rams player was suing the Patriots for allegedly taping the team's walkthrough practice sessions before Super Bowl XXXVI. This lawsuit was reported by the Boston Herald, after Matt Walsh, a former Patriots video assistant told them that Belichick ordered them to record the Rams' practice sessions, in particular the hand signals used by the defensive coaches. Goodell investigated this matter and he found out that though it was true that Walsh and the other Patriots' video team were present on the day the Rams had a walkthrough practice session, they were only there to set up video equipment for the game, and that there were no recordings made of the actual practice. This caused the Boston Herald to retract its previous report and issue an apology to the Patriots organization.

After the scandal and the imposition of penalties, Patriots owner Robert Kraft, and head coach Bill Belichick apologized to all the other team owners and head coaches, reiterating that the entire organization would be taking steps to make sure that nothing like this ever happens again.

The "Tuck Rule" Game

On January 19, 2002, the Patriots hosted the Oakland Raiders in the divisional playoff game. It was snowing that day in the former home of the Patriots, the Foxboro Stadium, so visibility was not the best. At the fourth quarter, the Raiders led the Patriots, and then the Charles Woodson of the Raiders managed to sack Tom Brady, causing him to drop the ball. The Raiders recovered the loose ball, and the only thing they needed to do to win the game was let the clock run out, but the referees overturned the play. They said Tom Brady's arm was actually moving forward at the time, so it was actually an incomplete pass and not a fumble; the officials noted the "tuck rule" as the basis for their call.

Ever since its inception in 1999, the Tuck Rule has always been controversial. According to the old NFL rule book:
NFL Rule 3, Section 22, Article 2, Note 2. When [an offensive] player is holding the ball to pass it forward, any intentional forward movement of his arm starts a forward pass, even if the player loses possession of the ball as he is attempting to tuck it back toward his body. Also, if the player has tucked the ball into his body and then loses possession, it is a fumble.

In other words, if the QB is bringing the ball forward in an intent to pass and he drops or loses it and it touches the ground, it is not a fumble, but is instead an incomplete pass. If the quarterback drops or loses the ball at any other time aside from the one already stated, then it is a fumble and the defensive team can recover the ball.

It is called the "tuck rule" because the forward motion is not necessarily an intention to pass the ball, the motion can also continue until the quarterback tucks the ball into his body to protect it. If the ball was tucked into the QB's body and he lost possession of it, then it is a fumble.

Tom Brady was not the only one to benefit from this rather flawed rule, in fact, the year before, the Patriots themselves have been on the receiving end of this kind of call in their match against the New York Jets. The reason why Brady's name is almost synonymous with the "tuck rule" is because it happened in such a pivotal game.

In 2013, during the NFL owners annual meeting in Phoenix, Arizona, the NFL finally abolished the rule via a 29-1 vote. The only team that was against abolishing the tuck rule was the Pittsburgh Steelers; the Patriots and Washington Redskins abstained. The tuck rule was replaced by a new rule that states: Passer Tucks Ball. If the player loses possession of the ball during an attempt to bring it back toward his body, or if the player loses possession after he has tucked the ball into his body, it is a fumble.

It might not be known if Tom Brady's involvement with the Tuck Rule had such an impact that led to the league scratching it out from the official rule book. However, one thing is for sure, Brady did bring more attention to the troublesome rule, so maybe he does hold some responsibility for it.

Deception

Just a week before the infamous Deflategate Game (which will be discussed in full later), the Patriots found themselves in another serious controversy. It happened during the semi-final game between the Patriots and the Baltimore Ravens. The head coach of the Ravens, John Harbaugh accused the Patriots of implementing a "substitution trick" that was tantamount to "deception" in his mind.

Here is what happened:

The Patriots, in an effort to keep the pesky Ravens defense off their backs, dug into their deep bag of tricks and lined up only four offensive linemen, and they declared the receiver, who was normally eligible, to be ineligible in an attempt to keep the Ravens defense confused and off-balance. Harbaugh got confused as to which of the Patriots on the field he needed to match coverage with. Harbaugh stated that it was a tactic that no one in the league had ever seen before, and that it was deliberately done to deceive them and that it was against the rules.
Tom Brady was having none of those accusations and fired back against Harbaugh. Brady said, "Maybe those guys [Harbaugh] got to study the rulebook and figure it out. We obviously knew what we were doing, and we made some pretty important plays. It was a real good weapon for us."

In the Patriots' defense, the play they used against the Ravens was technically within the rules and guidelines of the NFL, but it did push the envelope on what is considered "legal". The referee, Bill Vinovich, followed the usual protocol and used his discretion to decide on how much time the defense needed to react to substitutions by the offensive team. From the time of the substitution to the eventual snap, Vinovich allowed the Ravens roughly ten seconds to identify and adjust; any longer and it would be the Ravens who would get the unfair advantage. It was actually Harbaugh who was at fault for not calling a time out to properly give his defensive team assignments.

Deflategate

Probably the biggest scandal that the Patriots and Tom Brady have been embroiled in was the Deflategate controversy.

Deflategate is the term loosely used to describe the NFL's investigation on the allegations against the New England Patriots and its star quarterback Tom Brady. Not only did this controversy make the rounds within the NFL community, it got so huge and gathered quite a lot of drama that it became nationwide news, with almost all of the US's major news providers covering it and providing their own perspectives on the issue.

The investigation started in January 2015, and a final resolution was not reached until the middle of the next year, after a number of court hearings, countless press conferences, and an immeasurable number of plot twists and turns. The Deflategate controversy picked up steam quite quickly because the Patriots were slated to play in the next Super Bowl, which was the sixth one that the Brady-Belichick player-coach duo would participate in.

What sparked this investigation? There was a serious allegation that the New England Patriots had purposely used under-inflated footballs during their 2015 AFC Championship match against Peyton Manning and the rest of the Indianapolis Colts.

According to the NFL's rules, each ball used in professional games should be inflated to a standard range of 12 and a half to 13 and a half pounds per square inch. Each team is responsible for handing 12 game balls to the game referee for inspection, and furthermore, the home team is responsible for providing 12 backup balls.

According to ESPN correspondent Chris Mortensen's report on January 20, 2015, during the halftime inspection held by NFL personnel on the game balls used at the AFC Championship, 11 of the 12 balls provided by the Patriots for the game were under-inflated by a "significantly lower" amount, averaging to around 2 PSI each.

Several days after the report went out, the NFL announced that there would be an investigation held to find out if the Patriots deliberately tampered with the game balls after the AFC Championship match began. The league's decision to open up the investigation caused the days leading to that year's Super Bowl to be plagued with just one question: is the most successful team in the NFL full of cheaters?

What's the deal with under-inflated footballs, you ask? In theory, a football inflated below the standard PSI range gives the team a huge advantage. According to scientist and author of Newton's Football, Ainissa Ramirez, making the ball softer makes it easier to catch, hold, and throw; especially during a rainy day game, which was the weather condition during the fateful Patriots-Colts game.

Why did Deflategate become a national controversy? In simple terms, the Deflategate scandal had all the necessary elements to become a nationwide issue. First of all, the entire Patriots organization is not a stranger when it comes to controversies and NFL investigations.

Secondly, thanks to Tom Brady, the Patriots are the most winningest team in the 21st century. The Patriots eventually taking home the Vince Lombardi trophy after winning Super Bowl XLIX just days after the whole Deflategate investigations started made people question the integrity of the team. There was also the issue about the conversation and the reporting of the story. According to ESPN's report, 11 of the 12 balls presented by the Patriots were under-inflated, and this number turned out to be highly-inaccurate. After the NFL finished with its independent investigation, it turned out that only one ball was two PSI under-inflated.

Take all of these factors into consideration, and you get a recipe for the perfect storm of sports arguments. On one side, there are the people who say the Patriots are dishonest cheaters, and on the other, there are people who say that the Pats and Tom Brady are just victims of a witch hunt.

Finally, on May 2015, after extensive investigations, the NFL found out that it was "more probable than not" that it was the Patriots equipment managers who deliberately tampered with the balls used for the 2014-2015 AFC Championship game; however, the NFL also chose to suspend Tom Brady for four games, on the grounds that he knew what the equipment managers were doing and chose not to do anything to stop them. In addition, the Patriots were slapped with a $1-million-dollar fine, and they also forfeited their first and fourth round draft picks.

Robert Kraft accepted the punishment, but under protest. He said that he would reluctantly accept the NFL's decision, and stop further dialogue and rhetoric about the matter. But Tom Brady did not accept the decision, and he asked the court for an appeal to lift his suspension. One US District Judge actually sided with Brady, and he ordered the NFL to overturn Brady's suspension and let him play for the entirety of the 2015-2016 season. However, the NFL made a counter-appeal at the US Second Circuit Court of Appeals, who by a vote of 2 to 1, agreed that the NFL should uphold the suspension order on Brady. The only other option left for Brady and the NFL Player's union was to make an appeal at the Supreme Court. Brady, seemingly tired of all these legal battles, announced on July 15, 2016 that he would no longer pursue the matter and would not file an additional appeal.

Brady said that the past 18 months had been challenging, not only to him, but to his family as well, so he decided to no longer proceed with more legal action. He said that he would spend his suspension working even harder to become the best player that he can be, and that he would be looking forward to returning for the remainder of the season.

After sitting out the first four games of the 2016 regular season, Brady returned to lead the Patriots; and they would continue to win the Super Bowl that same season. However, even though the Patriots won the championship that year, the Deflategate scandal still haunted the team and made many people question their legitimacy as champions.

Tom Brady, despite being in the center of numerous controversies in his 18-year long career, does not seem to be fazed in the least. In fact, he treats every roadblock as a chance to make himself better, and that is just what he does.

Chapter 8: Tom Brady's Personal Life

Tom Brady's football life is quite a rollercoaster; he has experienced a lot of ups and downs, and has continued to prove his critics wrong. No movie scriptwriter could have ever imagined the kind of life Tom Brady had to go through before he became the household name he is right now. However, regardless of how colorful his football career has been thus far, his personal life can also be quite lively as well, and this is why many paparazzi stalk him on a regular basis.

The Original Brady Bunch… Where are they now?

True to his word, Tom Brady has risen to the top of professional sports and now the elder Brady sisters are known as "Tom Brady's sisters" and not the other way around. However, unlike Tom, the other Brady children did not pursue sports after graduating from college.

Maureen Brady, the eldest of the bunch, is currently married with two children of her own (Maya and Hannah). She is a school nurse and athletic director in their hometown of San Mateo. To this day, she never misses a single one of Tom's games; either she is in attendance at the stadium, or she will be watching the game live on the living room TV.

It also seems that Maureen's eldest daughter inherited her athletic genes. Maya, despite being a freshman at the Oaks Christian High School, has already committed to play for UCLA once she graduates. It seems like the legendary softball skills that her mother had have been transferred to her.

Julie Brady-Youkilis, the second eldest of the Brady bunch, used to play soccer for St. Mary's college, but she never took her sports career further than that. She became a special education teacher for a couple of years, but she is now a full-time mother of three kids. She is married to former Boston Red Sox baseman Kevin Youkilis, and has two kids with him, and another from a previous marriage. She still plays recreational soccer from time to time, and she also helps manage the craft beer brewing company set up by her husband after he retired from professional baseball.

Nancy Brady-Bonelli, the third eldest, is a health adviser at a research and consulting firm, and she is married to Steve Bonelli, a senior financial analyst for a real estate company. Although she earned a softball scholarship for the University of California, she opted to drop out and pursue a career that she felt she wanted more than sports.

Tom Brady's parents, Tom Sr. and Gallyn, are both enjoying their retirement in their old family home in San Mateo, where Maureen and her kids live as well. From time to time, they will try to watch a live game of their son, but they are more than happy to just see him on the television screen.

Unfortunately, Gallyn was diagnosed with Stage 2 breast cancer in 2016. She received several surgeries, and rounds of chemotherapy and radiation therapy to battle her aggressive form of cancer. That year, Gallyn was too sick to attend every single game of the New England Patriots, save one, Super Bowl LI, and it almost did not happen. Thankfully, Gallyn's doctors cleared her safe to travel just the day before her son led the Patriots team to win the biggest comeback game of his career.

The Bradys are still a very tight-knit family even now that all the kids have their own families. In fact, all of them came out in full force in 2012 for Julie's wedding. Tom came with his wife, supermodel Gisele Bundchen, and their kids. In addition, when the Deflategate scandal came about, you would see all of the Brady sisters come to the rescue of their little brother Tommy.

Tom Brady's Love Life

You would think that being a varsity football player in high school and college, Tom Brady would have a string of girlfriends, but that is not the case evidently. He really did not have time to date during his school years, and he has only ever been on the dating scene since he turned pro.

In 2002, fresh from his first Super Bowl win, Tom Brady dated former Playboy Playmate of the Year and actress Layla Roberts. However, their relationship never got past the dating stage. Roberts is now married to the founder of the now defunct AltaVista, John Hilinski.

Also in 2002, it was rumored that Tara Reid, one of the stars of the American Pie movie franchise, had a fling with Tom. In 2014, Reid admitted in an interview that she "had kissed" the NFL superstar, but she did not go into further details about their secret fling.

In 2004, Tom started dating actress Bridget Moynahan, and this became his first "official" romantic relationship. The press back then had a field day covering every move of the superstar couple. The pair were seemingly made for each other, but to everyone's surprise, they parted ways in 2006. In 2007, Moynahan would discover that she was three months pregnant with Brady's baby, and at the time Brady was already dating Gisele Bundchen.

In December 2006, just months after breaking up with Bridget Moynahan, Tom Brady started dating international supermodel Gisele Bundchen. Now, one would think that the two met in a swanky party exclusive only to the top celebrities, but the truth is that they met on a blind date set up by mutual friends. The two hit it off, big time. Even though Brady and Bundchen looked like the stereotypical athlete and supermodel couple, they are both very down to earth and genuinely love each other. The two tied the knot on 2009 in a very small, very private, and very simple ceremony in Santa Monica, California.

However, the two would also have a more public ceremony in Bundchen's estate in Costa Rica where all of their big name friends were invited.

Baby Mama Drama

The Brady-Bundchen love story was just in its infancy when news broke out that Brady's ex-girlfriend, Bridget Moynahan, was pregnant with his baby boy. Suffice to say, the entertainment press had a field day when the news leaked.

In a November 2015 interview, Bundchen told reporters that she actually considered running away from her and Brady's budding romance. Honestly, no one would fault her if she did. Bundchen confided that, at the time, she was really confused as to what to do; she was just months into this new relationship, but it had been going so well so far, but then she found out that her boyfriend's ex-girlfriend is pregnant with his child. Thankfully, the couple worked around their problems, and now, Brady is co-raising his son (John Edward Thomas Moynahan) with Bridget.

The New Brady Brood

Aside from his son with former girlfriend Bridget Moynahan, Tom Brady also has two more kids with his supermodel wife Gisele Bundchen; Benjamin Rein, who was born on December 2008, and Vivian Lake, who was also born in December, but in 2012.

As mentioned earlier, Tom co-raises his son John Edward Thomas (nick-named Jack). Although Jack has to travel between two homes, California with his mom, and Boston with his dad, it actually seems like the kid is growing up to be an upstanding young man.

Tom Brady's MAGA Cap

Tom Brady recently got into the media's crosshairs once again when the press caught a glimpse of a red Make America Great Again cap in his locker. The red MAGA Cap is one of the trademark symbols of Donald Trump's election campaign. The cap was seen during a post-game interview in 2015, when Donald Trump was still the GOP's Presidential candidate. When confronted about the MAGA cap, Tom Brady explained that he and Trump go back a long way. Back in 2002, Brady was in the judging panel of one of Trump's beauty pageants, and the pair hit it off almost right away.

Trump and Brady would regularly play golf together, and according to Brady, Trump would often call him and give him motivational speeches whenever he needed a boost. However, Brady did not clarify if he actually voted for Trump during the elections. One thing is for sure though, even though Trump has a lot of enemies in the NFL organization (players and administration people alike), there is one person that he will never badmouth ever, and that is Tom Brady.

Compared to all the things that Brady had to endure in his professional career, his life outside of football seems kind of bland, and that is just how he likes it. As much as possible, Brady likes to fly under the radar of the press, unless of course it is about his performance on the football field.

Chapter 9: What's Next For The GOAT?

The last trip of the Patriots to the Super Bowl was a massive disappointment for Tom Brady. The Patriots went into the post-season with an impressive 13-3 record, and were on a five-game winning streak. All that came crashing down when the Philadelphia Eagles blew past them in the fourth quarter of Super Bowl LII, outscoring the AFC champions by almost half.

This staggering loss for the forty-year-old, 18-year NFL veteran has cast a dark cloud over his imminent future. Will Tom Brady be retiring? Will he be leaving the New England Patriots? What's next for the GOAT?

Retirement News

Tom Brady will be turning 41 during the next NFL Season, and suffice to say, he seems still very spry and athletic for a guy his age. However, the years have definitely taken their toll. This is why rumors of his retirement have started circulating in mainstream media. Is Tom Brady retiring? If so, when?

In an interview with Oprah, Tom Brady talked about his plans regarding his retirement, and he said that he is actually thinking about it more now than ever. The end is "coming sooner, rather than later" according to the five-time NFL Champion. Oprah then asked Brady if there was a specific age that he had in mind for retiring, but he did not want to get into any specifics, as he was unsure of exactly when he would be hanging up his cleats for good. Brady said, "As long as I'm still loving it, as long as I'm loving the training [and] the preparation and [still] willing to make the commitment" he will still continue playing football.

In a separate interview on Good Morning America, Tom Brady said that his family will play a big part in his retirement plans, whenever the time comes of course. Brady said that these kinds of decisions are not necessarily just for oneself. "...the one thing that I've learned as I've gotten older [is that] there are collateral effects to every decision that I make." He then proceeded to talk about his wife (Gisele Bundchen) who still has a lot of aspirations and does a number of philanthropic works overseas. He also laments the difficulties of balancing raising three kids, his oldest living in California, while the other two are in Boston. However, Brady recognizes that he still has commitments with his team, more so now that they need him the most.

Even Bill Belichick was not spared by the media firestorm surrounding the rumored retirement plans of Tom Brady. However, during the annual meeting of the NFL in Orlando, Belichick said that the only information that he deems genuine will come from Brady himself. Belichick reiterates that Tom Brady and him have a very open line of communication; so, if Tom does decide to retire from football, he will be one of the first few people who will know.

Trade Rumors

Brady believes that no one is safe when it comes to the NFL, not even him. This is why he thinks that it is possible that he might retire as a player for another team other than the Patriots. In the past, the fear of getting traded to another team motivated Brady to work harder to improve his numbers, and he also agreed to several pay cuts just so the Patriots could still have room in the salary cap to work with.

However, with his age catching up to him, he says that he does not want to be a burden for the Pats. If Belichick and Kraft deems that it will be the best for the organization to let him go then he will acquiesce with the decision. However, knowing the close relationship that Brady has with Belichick and Kraft, and the legions of fans that he has, it is highly doubtful that Tom Brady will ever be seen wearing any team colors other than red, blue, and silver.

TB12sports.com and the TB12 Foundation

In 2016, Tom Brady launched his very own website, TB12Sports.com, which shows details about his rigorous training regimen. The website also has an online retail store where fans can purchase Brady merchandise. Later on, TB12Sports's online store expanded to include Brady's own healthy snack line, which contain raw, vegan, and organic ingredients that are completely free from dairy and gluten. This is a far cry from the unhealthy diet regimen that Brady followed when he was just starting at the NFL, and this just might be his secret to his strength and longevity in the physically demanding sport of American football.

Just a month after launching his website, Tom Brady, with the help of Boston Private and the Robert Paul Properties, formed the TB12 Foundation. The purpose of this non-profit is to provide free injury treatment, rehabilitation, and training for young, underprivileged athletes. As of writing, the foundation has helped dozens of underprivileged athletes, and they plan on helping even more.

On September 2017, Tom Brady published his very first book, The TB12 Method: How to Achieve a Lifetime of Sustained Peak Performance with the help of the Simon & Schuster publishing company. Within just two days of its release, Brady's book grabbed the number one bestseller rank on the Amazon best seller list, and also number 1 on the New York Times' weekly Best Sellers list.

Tom Brady certainly knows how to keep himself busy and active, so even if the retirement rumors that are making the rounds these days are true, you can be sure that he will still find a way to stay busy.

Conclusion

Love him or hate him, there is no denying the effect that Tom Brady has had on professional American football, and in the sports world in general.

Even after all of the scandals and controversies that Brady and the Pats have endured, his reputation is still well and truly intact. Even at 40 years old, he can still throw the ball as fast and as accurately as ever, and it does not seem like he will be slowing down any time soon.

Regardless of whether you are a fan of Brady or not, you cannot help but respect the man and his hustle. From being picked insanely late in the rookie draft, he rose through the ranks of the NFL to become the Greatest of All Time, and that should at least count for something.

Thanks once again for choosing this book. I hope that you've enjoyed learning about the incredible and inspiring life and career that Tom Brady has had!

www.ingramcontent.com/pod-product-compliance
Lightning Source LLC
Chambersburg PA
CBHW061103050726
47592CB00004B/1803